Walking Home from the Icehouse

Books by Vern Rutsala

The Window (1964)
Laments (1975)
The Journey Begins (1976)
Paragraphs (1978)
Walking Home from the Icehouse (1981)

Vern Rutsala

Walking Home
from the Icehouse

poems

Carnegie-Mellon University Press
Pittsburgh
1981
Feffer and Simons, Inc., London

Acknowledgments

PS
3568
·U83
W3

The American Scholar: "Visitors," *Bits:* "The Mill Back Home,"*Chariton Review:* "The Dog House," *Choice:* "The Broken Fields," *Esquire:* "Leaving England," *Harper's:* "The Furniture Factory," "Reedy's Galaxy," *Hudson Review:* "Access Road," *Massachusetts Review:* "American Dream," "Washrags," *Mississippi Review:* "Gravel, Roads, Fathers, Idaho, Hobos, Memory," *New England Review:* "The Icecold Freight," *New Letters:* "Pursuit," *The New Yorker:* "Walking Home from the Icehouse," *Northwest Review:* "Sunnyside Road after the War," "Visiting Day," "The New Life," *Ohio Review:* "The Journey Home," *Oregon Times Magazine:* "Lonely Roads," *Poetry:* "The World," "Moving West," "Going to War," *Poetry Northwest:* "On a Binge with Dakota Slim," *Poetry Now:* "Listening to Canadian Radio," "The Shack Outside Boise," "Errands for the Old Man," "Northwest Passage," "Words," *Poetry Texas:* "The Coast of Idaho," *Portland Review:* "Survey Party," *Rocket Candy:* "The War of the Worlds," *The Southern Review:* "Building the House," *Three Rivers Poetry Journal:* "The Other Road," "Something Like Spinks."

I want to thank the National Endowment for the Arts for a fellowship which helped me complete this book.

A number of these poems appeared in *The New Life,* a chapbook published by Trask House Books. Special thanks are due Carlos Reyes and Karen Stoner.

The publication of this book is supported by grants from the National Endowment for the Arts in Washington, D.C., a Federal agency, and from the Pennsylvania Council on the Arts.

Library of Congress Catalog Card Number 80-70566
ISBN 0-915604-47-7
ISBN 0-915604-48-5 pbk.
Printed and bound in the United States of America
First Edition

Contents

To Joan

The New Life

You wake with the taste of lost miles
of driving fast through dark mountains
of hairpin and horseshoe, of altitude
and icy air. Like a mist
sadness rides over. Was it a dream?
Like a mist it enters.
The pores of the house take it in.
You breathe it in like dust. And those figures—
shapes behind glazed windows—
ghosts? bit players from other nights?
You move, slow as a swimmer in strangeness.

This is all you have—
hard substance
ground to powder. Everything pulled
from your hands. Your own life too
like ash sucked up the chimney—
the tombs of China, your father's unmarked grave,
dust, dust, you move in strangeness.
You wake to oilcloth and linoleum.
You wake to the blemished mirror.
There is dust on everything. The secret
tops of books, piano keys, dimming
glistening leaves. The sad mist falls
like dew, like tiny grains for each eye.

Every day the same question in your mouth
for answer a sigh.
That great emptiness behind the stars
those huge clouds of cosmic dust
in their slow dance. You search the familiar
the way a man rips open
his wallet like a fish
to find his name.
Nothing, not even hangover, nothing.

You dress in strange garments
their touch soothing your hot skin.
And still that sense of travel, running in the night,
fear. Dust on everything, the house breathes it sighing.
You taste desert. Everything ground to powder.
You drift out to a street you've never seen.
Sunlight burns. You blink hard.
Frame houses, locust whirr
the sound of baseball in the distance.

It feels right. But the dust
keeps falling
dazzling in the sunlight, snowflakes of gold leaf.

You taste the cold desert. The houses shrivel.
Everything ground to powder. The body knows.
Bones pulverized
to make the flour that makes the bread
the giant eats.

The Shack Outside Boise

They have brought you here
where a fine brown silt
covers everything. You want
to ask about color
but it is too late.
They have taken that away.
You eat your brown food
with your brown spoon
and talk softly
with your dark cousins, their
bony arms starved thinner
by shadow. You see the sadness
they call possesssions,
the helpless objects
they brought here with great effort—
old generators, bald tires,
a trunk full of mildew,
slaughtered mountains
of the broken and useless.
Then slowly in the exhausted light
they divide it up
making sure you get your fair share.

The World

I move back by shortcut
and dream. I fly above
it all, the dark stain
where swamps soak up
the lake's extravagance,
stubble hills, the valley's
green finger. This is the place
of pure invention, secret
as old wood
under a hundred coats
of paint. I invent
my own way back, invent
these wings, this
Piper Cub of tissue paper
I glide in, circling the valley
chasing my shadow across
the lake, twisting each layer
back through air.
The town scatters out
along the highway and I cut low
buzzing the school, signaling
my old teachers' chalky bones.
I bank away approaching town
along the old road
that rises from a low plain
where the land tastes bad,
where dust even slips
under rich men's doors.
I trace it like a route
on a map and it climbs
kept company by a creek
with a mouth full of boulders.

I finger wind for updrafts
slowing above the dump,
then sweep around the lake,
past Indian Village
and summer homes,
steering hard I top
the mill, my steering wheel
an old lard can lid
on the end of a stick,
my seat a log set back
in the woods, the shade cool
and safe in the arc cut
by the rope swing
thirty years ago.

American Dream

I listen hard in the kitchen
Any sound is welcome
The cars go by the late drinkers
The dragass lovers
I listen until one car stops
I look out
It's the old Ford
Trailing vines and garbage
Back from the junkyard
Decorated with dents and rust
Windshield shattered to milk
Cavities where the headlights were
What prodigies of effort
Brought it here
Struggling without gas without tires
But it's back
Terribly risen
Risen and drawn here
Like a dog in a story

On A Binge With Dakota Slim

I pick a year, say 1932
and travel back by hearsay,
back to the old kitchen
with its glass of spoons
in the exact middle
of the table.
We are there together
letting it all get too much
for us, letting it all build up,
sitting night after night
with only two sounds—
her radio, our steady honing.
The snick and whirr,
the static straight from Boise
and every blade already
keen enough for surgery.
How much coffee can you drink?
How sharp do knives have to be?
It's one of those times
we dread and long for—
the cold bedroom, the single bed,
getting up at five
to work the pond.
(We're like cats on those logs.)
But it's all too much for us.
How much kindling can you chop?
It's one of those clockwork times—
three months gone and time
to get the hell out,
time to trade that whetstone in
on the rusty edge
of bootleg booze.

Think we'll go into town, we say
and get out
just before the skillet hits the door.
Woman's got a hell of an arm, we say.
In town we hear the skillet ring
and let the first drink
slide down slow as summer weather.
That's a little better, we say,
just a leetle better now.
Let the goddamn radio
dim those blades dull again
we don't care. We're here
and by god we'll stay
until we drink our paycheck dry.

The Journey Home

Alone, in the rain, hungover
                    you come back.
On foot
          in cardboard shoes, in a thin
Cheap jacket, in a hat
                    without shape
You make your way.
                    You come back to this house
Long past flowers and cards,
                    long past salesmen
Pacing square feet,
                    long past buyers
With the eager eyes of thieves.
                              Long past funerals,
Long past grief's great stone
                    and healing's dream,
Long past all this
          you come back to vacancy,
To broken windows
          to spiders and rats
To the flurry of startled birds
                    to dust and debris
And a broken toy
          you come back
And pound and pound
                    on this locked door.

Washrags

In Long Valley the Finns
Brought the old country with them
Brought it in the 'nineties
In steerage in their ragged luggage
They lugged it with them
It was a millstone and the knives in their boots
It was the way they stood around
The store in town
Eyes down shoulders hunched
Waiting for everyone else to buy
They packed it with them in gunny sacks
They took it to dances
Condensed and distilled
In pint bottles
They beat each other with it
Behind Finn Hall
Its weight pulled
Them out of school at fourteen
It ruined their teeth with hardtack
And filled their mouths
With strange accents
No soap would wash loose
It was the broken axle and the bad crop
It was the huge tree
They knew would fall
They smiled grimly
Knowing 1929 by its real name
It let the travelling dentist
Pull all my grandfather's teeth
The year he died
It was in the washrag I buried
For my father
to cure a wart

Building the House

Among shadows and pieces,
the scraps of old houses,
I clear a place, tamping earth
flat, and draw a plan
in the dirt. I lean toward
the old house, that long vacancy
and scar where it stood,
that address of absence.
Out of nothingness and shadow
I try to build it up again.
I begin with kindling
and mill ends. I use
the cardboard tools of memory.
How was this room? I feel
my way along a floor, fingers
remembering. I try again
to revive each board,
remember it into being
and with effort hold it in mind
until it falls in place beside
the others and the nails slip in
soundless as pins. Under way now
the walls rise, every board
finds its place, each one a word
each wall a page, and the rooms
come back easy as sunrise
revealing each oval picture,
each square of old linoleum.
One by one they add themselves,
darkness brushed away like cobwebs—
the house new and old at once,
fresh nails in blond wood
bleed rust down flaking paint.

Holding it in mind I move
through its lives—sawdust
of newness, sag of neglect,
weeds of abandonment.
It breathes back and forth
as I breathe, my breathing
keeping it alive. I put in
windows and replace the matchstick
rafters. I add shadows
to the corners and scoops of dreams
for each bedroom. Holding my breath
I deliver all the cheap furniture
at once. I put everything
in place like a watch—
my ship in a bottle, memory's toy—
until it's nearly ready, swept
new again and waiting
for its family. Lamplight strokes
the trees alive, smoke dreams
from the chimney. Finally
I add the brass knob,
then enter and meet
the cold music of empty rooms.

Sunnyside Road After the War

Ancient flypaper curls in winter
light and I drive back
over all those gravel roads
through dead farms, land sucked dry,
scorched grass the pale
memory of crops. I hear guitars,
amplifiers tuned high,
as toothless singers
cry of careless
love and wildwood flowers.
I remember the oily windows
blurring amber as I fell asleep.
I fall asleep that way again
and hear the whooping
name of that parched summer,
boozed yodels daring
the night to end.
And again they look for jobs,
look on all the wrong streets,
knock on all the wrong doors
and wind up in the sick
light of waterfront bars.
What the hell, you
can always use a shovel
for the county.
August's fires died, rain
filled ditches, their clunkers
wouldn't start, strings broke.
They sat in their shacks, the war
was over, they strummed, caught colds
and watched the stiff brims
of their beautiful hats
go gray and limp.

Visiting Day

Dark presence, old crow, hag
face at the window
our wrists are icy with your grip,
our tongues go numb.
Take these flowers, this candy.
We're muffled, your shawl
covers us all, we see
through its weave only—
helpless, tall as we are, helpless
remembering the dark places
you studied into being
inside each of us—lesson after lesson,
detail upon detail. And none
could run far enough.
One fled eating great handfuls
of scripture. She is here, submissive,
a good girl now. Another
took a wife but your icy fingers
held his genitals tight
and small as a baby's.
He is here, too, shy as a boy,
hair combed flat and wet.
Others stayed close, drawn
by your dark fire, and suffered
the twisted kiss of abscess and ache,
haywire age gobbled them
early. Still others you
pumped up with fat—
they ate and ate searching for the food
you never served.
They loll here now, wheezing
nibbling peanuts, eyeing your forbidden candy.
What did you want?

We offered our torn flesh
for patches, we swallowed
every button you offered.
What did you want?
We've allowed our brains
to curl tight as a rat's,
curled like the meat
in a nut, like the core of a golf ball.
What did you want?
It took years—diplomas,
certificates, even prizes—
believe me it took years.
We know the maze.
Was this it, old rip?
We moved in the shallows,
in the school districts
of middle age. We wore
dark suits and combed our hair.
Was this it?
You knit. We're lifted still
with the skein, we feel the needles
in and out, in and out.
But what is enough?
Told to love lies
we loved them. No one
crossed his fingers. No one.
And no one should doubt us.
The lies were lovely—intricate,
of durable materials.
But no one believed us.
We wept—as we weep now
here with these flowers.

To atone we were given small whips
made of our mothers' hair.
Punish yourselves, a voice said, a voice
like yours. Punish yourselves
we have no time.
Our knees were raw with thanks.
We developed the art of the welt.
We favored the baroque—
are you listening?—
we favored the baroque
and scoffed at impressionism.
There were one or two cubists.
They were despised.
Did you see that?
Did you approve? Was it worth
a few cookies? The kind with raisins
we spent our dark childhoods
pretending to like?
This was all for you.
We obeyed ourselves into debt.
We followed rules
until our feet were bloody.
All for you. All for you.
We have done what we can.
The dead bring their bones,
the living their nerves loose
as old clothesline, bunged up and loony,
older than you, cackling crazy and senile.
We bring sickbeds and credit cards,
we bring blindness and candy.

The Mill Back Home

Logs drowse in the pond
Dreaming of their heroes
Alligator and crocodile

Reedy's Galaxy

On summer nights
The south wall
Of Tim Reedy's
Tarpaper shack
Looked like a sky
Full of stars
Lamplight
Shining through
The countless
Tiny holes
He put there
Killing flies
With his silver .22

The Other Road

Where the asphalt runs off the page
I begin

At the county line
The road buckles with pain

Its shape dictated in spring
By wheels by boots

By whatever can gouge
With summer it sets

Like a twisted ribbon of sculpture
Delivering up the potholes

Earned last winter
This is our road

The one we're told to take
They make it tough

But we expect nothing easy
None of those humming interstates

Without a seam
None of those cobblestones

Set like jewels
This is our road

We voted it in
We elected this road for its looks

And because no one else
Dares use it

It's a road for donkey carts
And asses like us

We like it
We go this way every night

Because it always takes us home

Visitors

Speck on the map that it was
The town seemed big
Some swirled place near the center
Somehow the right place
And we expected the famous to come
And they did every one
Aimee Semple McPherson
Closed all the bars for a day
And that went into our talk on the corner
Picked over like a Christmas turkey
Until we got thirsty
There was that long summer
With its list of the famous
Robert Young Spencer Tracy Walter Brennan
Though among those actors
The general favorite
Was Isabel Jewell
Yes we knew that if they knew
Everyone would come
And they did one by one
Water ski champs and donkey baseball
Even the tallest man in the world
His apple box shoe
Displayed with bunting
In the drugstore window
A handsome man
A lawyer they said

Though we thought
Being that tall
Was job enough for anyone
We chewed over these legends
On the corner
And felt the justice
In their coming to see us
We knew we counted
We knew we were a secret center
And knew the visitors
Would live here too
If they could
Only the Globetrotters
Left a strange frenzy
No one could quite handle
And for years after
The town team was poor
The boys all arms and legs
The ball a stranger in their hands

Words

We had more than
we could use.
They embarrassed us,
our talk fuller than our
rooms. They named
nothing we could see—
dining room, study,
mantel piece, lobster
thermidor. They named
things you only
saw in movies—
the thin flicker Friday
nights that made us
feel empty in the cold
as we walked home
through our only great
abundance, snow.
This is why we said 'ain't'
and 'he don't'.
We wanted words to fit
our cold linoleum,
our oil lamps, our
outhouse. We knew
better but it was wrong
to use a language
that named ghosts,
nothing you could touch.

We left such words at school
locked in books
where they belonged.
It was the vocabulary
of our lives that was
so thin. We knew this
and grew to hate
all the words that named
the vacancy of our rooms—
looking here we said
studio couch and saw cot;
looking there we said
venetian blinds and saw only the yard;
brick meant tarpaper,
fireplace meant wood stove.
And this is why we came to love
the double negative.

Northwest Passage

Out past Sylvan Beach is the place
They still call Indian Village
Built only to be burned
The summer Spencer Tracy came to town

For years after that
Whole families would picnic there
Scavenging the debris
For rubber arrowheads

But when Spencer came
Everyone got jobs
Five dollars a day and lunch
The Depression ending with glamour

And the chance to sew on a button
For a star
Some of the men were extras
Growing beards and wearing buckskin

Rogers' Rangers looking for that passage
All summer long
From eight to five
My father was among them

And once years later
The summer after he died
I saw the movie on the late show
I stared at it hard

Even recognized a few landmarks
I scavenged every frame
For the smallest sign of him
I found none

Errands For the Old Man

I've been rummaging all
My attic lumber
The attic I always carry
But it's too late now
I have all these things
A maple bar
In a spotted sack
Ten penny nails a can of gas
A hopeless quart of raspberry ripple
And two copies of *Ring Magazine*
What do I do with these things
Why do I have them
I can't even give them away
Why did you send me for them
And why
Why on earth did I never
Bring them back to you

The Icecold Freight
for Kathe

Thirsty, I turn the radio on
letting noise fill my gaps—
a country music whine,
that studs and shiplap sound,
that skeleton of feeling,
old nails pulled from boards.
Old man, father, whatever
your name, I swim
back through dust
and wood chips, back
to the summer we built
a house together and beyond,
deeper, the time you grew
a beard. I remember
the straight razor slicing
your chin. I remember
the scar you carried
to death.
        Tonight
I want everything in—
frost slowly forming
on the car roof
as if the streetlight
scattered a kind of talcum;
my homemade valentine
dangling from the light cord;
and the undertaker's breath,
pre-sweetened, his ashtray filled
with paperclips.
        Coffee boils,
I sit back and drink
its darkness, hard times
falling with the ice.

We're taking our own
medicine again, those small
bitter pills doled out
by persimmon-faced
nurses. Hard times
music like that throb
you carried all your life,
that Depression war wound—
how the world went
cold and gray, how it
would go that way again.
You knew that icecold
freight was on the way
and knowing made you gunshy
and careful with a hammer.
There were no second chances,
a nail gone was
a nail spent.
            I listen now
to truck stop
music getting everything
in, singing of lost
farms and the dead—
echoes, gristle music.
With your wound you
took your time that
summer. I hated
slowness and every board.

Victim of the miter box
you checked and checked,
carpenter's pencil scrawling
over every two-by-four,
testing each deceptive
number. You thought
nature lied, in cahoots
with politics. Nothing should be
easy and every calculation
must be triple-checked.
In the way and useless,
despising the dry ground,
I longed for trips
to the little store for cokes
and cupcakes and slow talk
in the cool interior
with the crazy owner.
But you kept at it
and slowly a house
rose from nothingness.
                    The music
goes on, on the edge—
like Humbird and Wiebe
in their shacks that summer,
guitars filling dusty
air with song. They played
and played and sometimes
brought over a beer
and helped lift the rafters,
half drunk but willing.

The war was over, jobs
were hard to find
and the icecold freight
churned through those
summer fields. But
the house rose, bit by bit—
almost finished when
we moved in, tarpaper
and half a floor.
That winter we froze
and I hated it
but tried to swear
and cough like you,
tried to bang around
the kitchen mornings
before school—and played
football hard, knowing nothing
was easy.
          In the music
I hear your saw
whine, sense your tack hammer
on the roof in little
beats. Frost is gone,
rain falls the way it did
that year when the oil heater
never gave enough heat
and I ran to the kitchen
to get dressed.
Now rain eases, ghost blossoms
unclench in strangeness.

I feel the old chill,
the hard times throb.
The neighborhood was desolate—
shacks and tents and not
a tree in sight. Like
the music Wiebe and Humbird
twanged every night
until I went to sleep.
Ancient summer uncovers
ancient summer—your
beard, your razor cut,
your scar—memory
travelling back and forth,
pacing through another rain
in hipboots and galoshes.
Buds nudge and die
in cold, the city lops trees
to stumps, and that far-off
house endures the weather
still, held up with nails
my irritation pounded
home.
        Monument enough for you—
worried into being by
your flat pencil and your
curses, a place to live,
no shrine. I learned this
and then forgot and now
it comes back: The cutting board,
the thumbed book, the worn
furniture speak our lives to us.

And I wonder if
the handmade backboard you
put up still stands.
The net shredded off
the hoop the first year
but I used it hard,
working on my left hand
hour after hour. You sighed
and swore that scarecrow
structure up as well—for me—
another monument of use
and the need to learn
Joe Fulks' jump shot.
And for a while we kept
the icy freight off
that street. It was music
and shacks and hot
summers, football and baskets.
The radio says it's lonely
time and I believe it.
The radio sobs and whimpers,
tough guys ground
to jelly. They know, they know.
With Wiebe and Humbird
I switch to wine, fed up
with unemployment checks
and coffee. Ghost trees
haunt the neighborhood. Money
for a sixpack turns up

under a flat rock. Hope
tunes our strings and pays
light bills. But we
wake to tarpaper and tents,
to empty cupboards
and jobs likely
as a royal flush.
                    The icecold
freight warms up nearby
and its diesel fouls
our summer, the bad news
only war can cure.
The freight snorts and paws
like a bull, needing us.
And Truman, you said, shuffling
his deck finds some action
in Korea, and the summers
disappear. A brother of the freight
scattering dollars pulls in,
wheezing red steam. We
still live with that lukewarm
freight that mulches
everything. Humbird and
Wiebe and I listen to your
music, remembering. The old
house turns monument
and lost, and, father,
                    I
see you in your railed bed.

I trim your fingernails—
there's nothing else to do.
Your hands are thin, I.D.
bracelet so loose on your wrist.
We built a house together!
The radio sings lugubrious—
I go all the way back again,
touch that summer, that scar,
vow a beard no matter what,
dream guitars and sun,
dream hammers and studs,
dream that house from nothingness
again—our monument,
the one I hated every inch of,
the one we built together.

Survey Party

We stumble all over the county
Lining things up
Truing property
We knock down fences
And let fields marry for love
We divvy up the rich men's pies
We divide and subdivide
Fine-chopping smooth estates
To postage stamps
It's a wonderful night
And we work hard
For equipment
Sixpacks and wine
And not a plumb-bob in sight
Oh it's a wonderful night
We stumble all over the county
And come up
With a cockeyed version
They'll have to live with
Oh we gerrymander the hell
Out of everything

Something Like Spinks

Now I stay awake to dream.
I invite the old times in
and they arrive clean,
free of travel grime
so honed down they're
only bone and ink,
flat dreams the needle
of the pen withdraws. That girl,
I don't even remember
her name, something like Spinks,
and the town's wild man,
Dingaling Red. They're here now
come back in pieces, free
of cosmoline, come back from air
and the rust of thirst.
She was a neighbor's cousin
from the farm—a farm
I saw once: cowshit
hip deep in the yard,
everything falling down.
He even called himself that,
proud of the title, Dingaling Red,
father of a friend who ate
with us and often spent the night—
a frightened little blackhaired kid
called Wart. They're all here now
insisting, faces through a fog.
She was older, maybe twelve.
She was skinny but strong
and she had a mean streak
but mainly I remember
how she rode on the pickup's
front fender, one hand on
the radiator cap, feet on the bumper.

For a while Red owned a bar
with whorehouse attached
but he went broke, gambling
and drinking his face
red as his hair. He didn't
seem to care. She rode on the fender—
it was a big family or maybe
the truck bed was full
of cowshit. Anyway that's how she rode
her ugly old man squirrelling
all over those backcountry washboards
driving like the damned fool he was
trying to make her flinch.
When they wheeled in spitting gravel
she hit the ground running
and swearing. It was a fine
thing to see. And when they left
she sat there so casually
with style and a kind of whipcord spirit
like she knew exactly what it meant.
I remember Red grinning and winking
and how his laugh seemed raw red too.
He died in a fiery wreck
and for a week the slow
drivers felt pleased with themselves
but then the beer went flat,
the war began and things
were never quite the same again.
About the girl—you know the story—
something happened and she fell off
and was killed. Everyone
said it would happen some day
and it did.

Listening to Canadian Radio

It's time for country miles
The buzz of words
The fishbones of broken lines
I clear the round table
Go over it with a sponge
Searching the swirled grain
For my face your face
The wings of fabulous birds
I remember the fury
Of Run Sheep Run
And then it's gone
No matter how
I fiddle with the dial
The whole town lost in fog
Static and fadeouts like memory
Gliding to Idaho
And back again
Then Nanaimo comes through
Listing people I once knew
The dim signal travelling south
Scraped almost inaudible
On trees and mountains
Travelling south as I move east
Over Cabbage Hill
Looking in the night
For the ancient place
Riding one clear note
Through foggy sound
To the very edge
Of that lost town

Gravel, Roads, Fathers, Idaho, Hobos, Memory

We move slowly now over gravel,
the last hint we've had of roads
in this long search for our fathers.
We hope this place is Idaho
as we were told by hobos
so far back in our memory

it's nearly lost. Or is this memory
we touch and only think it's gravel,
our path more lost than any hobo's?
Perhaps we've followed too many roads
as imaginary as the place called Idaho
where they said we would discover fathers.

But still we are without fathers
except those fading images in memory
who invented this wilderness of Idaho.
Soon enough we'll eat the gravel,
soon enough we'll abandon roads
and jungle-up forever with the hobos.

Or do we dream the hobos
as we dream our lost fathers,
night after night along these roads?
There is something in our blood, a memory
grinding like gears to produce this gravel
we scatter like seeds all over Idaho.

Give us a break, we're lost, Idaho!
We can't even find those old hobos,
and quarry as we will there's too little gravel
for the single file we need to reach our fathers!
We're drunk, confused, our memory
bulldozed and gouged by new roads.

We travel circles, not roads
and have never admitted Idaho
to the union, much less our memory.
And we carry within us strange hobos
who all insist they are our fathers
in voices harsh as gravel.

So we give up roads and gravel
and every memory of dim hobos
who lied of Idaho and our fathers.

Access Road

Slowly at first, dully
I begin to look,
feeling my way along the edge
of town, fingering the city limits
for flaws, looking for some
hole in the wire,
some gap in district lines
and soon I'm out,
slipping through a crack
in the zoning laws,
out and gliding low
over dewy meadows,
heading fast for Idaho,
remembering those old summer nights
clear as a bell and cold as hell.
I beat the bushes,
I run my hand over surfaces
feeling for gravel,
picking up dirt and sniffing
for the old volcanic smell,
searching for any hint
searching for the old road
to the farm
long overgrown, long ago
given back to the woods.

I worm my way across posted fields.
I trespass on government lands
past storage dumps
and oil pumps, clawing
my slow way
until like the secret source
of a river
a few pebbles signal
the beginning.
They rattle like dice.
They are my precious gems
and soon they increase.
I walk crunching the gravel,
holding my breath for the bend in the road,
the bend that promises
and withholds everything.

The Coast of Idaho

Late at night we heard waves
suffering their slow
way from Oregon,

crawling the dust like snails,
scaling mountains, scuffling
through gulches

until we felt them in the lake
where our monster drowsed
waiting for the perfect weekend

when he would make us famous
in a Sunday supplement.
He knew the sea

and in him we knew it too.
He was an exile
from that green regime

and now he farmed our lake
masquerading as a deadhead
winking those old knotholes

in the moon-inspired waves.
Winters he spooned the arctic in—
our dogs turned white,

our dark bears
erased themselves with snow—
but the sea was always there

lapping in that inch of air,
urged across all those miles
from Coos Bay,

moving like an oyster
then surfacing again with spring,
our scoop of sea

our pool of sky
containing all the images—
the green deep,

the giant bear trap clams
of South Sea movies,
U-boat sharks

patrolling each dream,
water tigers, sea elephants
and the caped ray

cloud shadow, devil fish—
all piped into our lives
underground, by radio

and double features twice a week.
Our water glass vision
of the sea came in, a log

wearing a halloween mask,
calling our names in sleep,
pumping our blood all night.

Walking Home
From the Icehouse

I pack in for the night
Carrying whatever I need
In pockets and clipboard
Culling the exits for ripeness
Trying the bus marked AGE
Heading for the icehouse
I do the opposite
                 of take
Remembering the way
                     in pieces
The path no wider
               than a string
Every spring
           the meadow by the icehouse
Overflowed
         killdeer
               moss smothering
Surfaces
        tadpoles dotting the clear water
But the access road
              dwindles
Down again
          becoming this path
I scratch
       through the deepest woods
I know
     The trees like a wall
Some green marble sweating
Bears and wildcats
Once we walked those
Marbled veins
Wandering a thickness
Suddenly lithe
Spidery with ferns
Alone I knew

The softness stiffened
And lost me like a door
Slammed shut
A closet of faces and fingers
And hot whispers
At your back
Anything could happen then
The floor go limp with snakes
And the air grip
Like muscles in a throat
With the wildcat's screech and thump
The one orange word the woods spoke
Screaming wild
                    locking the door
I drop to my hands and knees
Crawling under ferns
                         until
I touch ancient toys
Trucks and tractors
                     just blocks of rust
I find old clothes
                  a tiny
Checked jacket
I find rings
And ticket stubs
A waterlogged yearbook
Old furniture comes apart
                          in my hands
We caught tadpoles in mason jars
And now
         I walk that way again
Past the icehouse
                  and the road to school
Bob and Ruth and I
Soaked to the waist

Limp flowers
In our hands for bribes
We pass George Buck's
George who nursed
                    his sick heart
Home from town
                    twice a week
I see him walk
                then pause
Counting to sixty
He's back there as we pass
Bouquets wilting
                    pants icy
                        on our thighs
He made the finest bows
Strings so tight
                they hummed
Now I'm sifting hard
Wilderness all around
Darkness smothering my skin
I pick up baby teeth like pennies
Lost hair like pins
So dark
        my eyes are pebbles
We shiver
            in the chill
Dreading the fever
        of kitchens
The quick heat
                of scolding air
And their father's
                tantrums
The walk is always longer than you think
It takes us by Harry Culp's
Empty house
                large and shady
So much deeper than our houses

And his toys
          were numerous with delight
But they did no good
I remember his pale skin
And the way his
          tiny arms
              jutted
From shirts
          that always seemed too big
Older
     he reached
          our size again
Then grew smaller
          shrinking back
To babyhood to please
          his aging parents
The last time
He was like
          a sack of ivory kindling
In his father's arms
          lost in the huge
Folds of striped
          overalls
          head lolling
Loose as a baby's
          engineer's cap
             askew
I leave this neighborhood
This room
This paper
I leave the dark city
And my neighbors
          all those sleeping
            irritants
I leave this and pack in

All the way
All the way
          to the broken fields
Of fathers and sons
The dark nights of coughing
The sounds of morning
As he banged fire
                from the iron stove
Now we hurry by the Culps's
And I drop off Bob and Ruth
And slip home
Down the hill
                hearing their father say
He'll tan their
                skinny little asses
Now I flinch
          past swamp
And hopeless mason jars
Tadpoles bleak soup
                    in sunlight
Past the icehouse and the road to Boise
The exit from trees
                  and freedom
Everyone said Bob's and Ruth's father
Was as cocky
              as a banty rooster
And it was true
                  He stood that way
Stocky and straight
                  chin high
                        handy with his fists
Later
      as the war moved us west
And we forgot the town
I saw him in bed

          just milk leg
He said
Bob and Ruth looked scared
We had little to say
Later still
          we heard his mind
Went
He visited home sometimes
Playing in the yard
Like a three year-old
His children's
          youngest brother

The Dog House

Homesickness draws us in.
We want those caverns
in a glass, that music
of alleys filled with
one-eyed toms and loggers
crippled sick with booze.
We need the homesick lies
in those songs. We want the hilarity
of broken hearts, of silver dollars

winking in a cardroom, slot machines
sucking dimes. We buy it all
from Miss Kitty behind the bar,
buy winter in frosted mugs
and tonight it's all there again—
the safe underwater gloom, faces
passing you like fish, you note
the teeth of sharks, wolf shadows,
the titter of minnows.

You idle in the sway tasting
all the fuming echoes—
boilermakers and sweat, majorettes
all gratitude and legs
after the big win.
It all turns delicate as spray
and you weave, its dew on your tongue,
shedding old skins, fiddles
nagging the new man out,

guitars polishing the skin transluscent—
everything shining through
until you see souls like pickled embryos,
those tiny gray fists
in everyone like crumpled bait.

You keep at it now
in too deep to fight the current,
keep at it until
the dog team sign climbs down

and sets off whining
for the winter hell of Idaho,
jackpots everywhere
raining icy silver.
You ride the legend of their tracks
as tonight's murmur rises high,
singing of how things end, must end.
How the owners lost the place
and trickled off to Reno

and suicide when liquor by the drink
came in and everything else
was against the law.
But we were there again tonight
breathing lightly in that sea,
chewing our crooked hooks, remembering
the old house rules:
For the big winners—rooms upstairs;
for losers, split lips and broken jaws
and home, tail between your legs.

Pursuit

And now I follow my father
For three years
Living on crackers
Drinking from puddles
I bide my time
Watching
As he shadows the three
Who beat hell out of him
Behind Finn Hall
It is my job
I must do it right
Salty crackers biting
The sores on my tongue
Winter turning my feet
To stumps
But I hang on
As one by one
He catches them
And makes them pay

Going to War

This trip I ignore the bypass,
searching for the old road
they gave back to the grass—
not even second-hand now,
fit only for the rusty ghosts
of Model-A's and Hudsons,
the crippled heaps up on blocks
still limping toward jobs
in the shipyards
thirty years too late.
You find such roads behind
billboards, ambling slowly away
to a nothingness in weeds.
No one remembers them
or those pioneers hobbling west
in '42, Depression wolves
nipping blowouts from their heels.
They dreamed along the old
highway, the last flakes
of the farm blowing back,
the black stove icecold.
It was cities from now on
and they paved over
their acres forever. I see us
beside the old roadster,
background drifts of snow
in the Blue Mountains.
We're still at peace
between Idaho
and Coos Bay. As we drive
I watch the clear sky,
the swoop and rise of wires.

Snow is familiar, no part
of war, but in Coos Bay
we see the strange ocean
colder than snow.
The gray water seems dull
except for the sound,
those regular salvos
and the thought of Japan
out there. We stay a week
and I feel the ocean-damp
in my bed, chew sand in my food—
big-necked clams like the sea
signalling power and ugliness.
Darkness droops low, some
chill shadow around us
like muddy water
and every mile to Portland
brings the chill closer,
our car using up the last
of peace and Idaho.
I feel the war enter
as we enter the city's
dusty fringe, squeezing
everything down to a cold
key in my chest. The war
happens then, the one
that never ends.

The Furniture Factory

Upstairs the sanders
rubbed fingernails
thin, hands shiny
and soft as a barber's—
men past forty
down on their luck.
Below, I worked in a haze
of fine dust
sifting down—
the lives of the sanders
sifting down, delicately
riding the cluttered
beams of light.
I pounded nails
on the line.
The wood swallowed hard
nailheads like coins
too thin to pick up.
During breaks I read—
You gonna be
a lawyer, Ace?—
then forgot the alphabet
as I hammered
afternoons flat.
My father worked there too
breathing the sanding
room's haze.
We ate quiet lunches together
in the car.
In July
he quit—hands
soft, thick fingernails
feathery at the tips.

The Broken Fields

The poverty of night and summer
The slow motion of your blood
Turn up the only theme
Your song these nights
                    coughed up
With cigarettes and beer
In the nearest tavern
                brought home
Like some behind the bar
Souvenir
        Some guilt wrapped
In cellophane
You sit drinking coffee now
Working your mind thin as a wire
With sounds
            and houses broken up
For kindling and parking lots
Thinking hard
You put out spoons and bowls
For the children
And this is when you're caught
You feel your slow way back
Through the wilderness
Of your father's life
               reaching deep
To pry loose his dreams
And find yourself
            sleeping there

But it's ended
There is nothing to learn
You only fumble toward the same
Betrayal
          your own dirty spoon and bowl
And nights when no one
Keeps the rafters still
With his bare hands
                    or brings
The drink that cures
Bad dreams

The War of the Worlds

So many things happen
on trips yet all we
remember is middle—
start and finish burned
away, lost like pencil
points and erasers.
But this is okay.
Memory lights up
that old stretch of road
and I feel the rough
upholstery of my back
seat corner. They've turned
on the radio and I hear
the invaders advance on
Princeton, New Jersey—
a place much farther than
Mars—hear the speaker
conjure the pylon shadow
with panic, then
the spitting sound
of things being crushed
followed by silence,
that beautiful ominous
silence yawning all the way
to Idaho and filling
our small car with echoes.
I feel very calm
and invisible. The world
is more interesting
than I had been led
to believe. I think we'll
survive—they never mention
Idaho on the radio.

And there are no shadows,
only green hills and meadows
and the men's airless calm—
my father and his friend
saying "war" with proper
respect, my mother calm
and interested too,
but the other woman
suddenly hysterical, crying:
"My babies! My babies!"
Childhood's usual embarrassed
witness I am sad at this
and concentrate politely
on the view, pleased
with my insignificance
and sure no invasion is worth
such tears and foolishness.

Leaving England

Late now I follow old roads.
Gravel bites my feet.
I feel the old mystery
of culverts, the strangeness
of switchbacks and winding.
I follow one to the dump.
Another leads to the swamp
where I dredge night after night.
My dreams fill up with silt.
In sleep I travel home—
under sail, in steerage, week
after poisonous week—to waste
spaces, backroads, the unmapped
plains of hunger. My shovel
digs sod. All the travelled miles
scale down to cold wind,
the whine of aching space.
I move in darkness
nudging like a mole
through that sandy history,
all that rocky soil.
I move by rumor,
by the uneven spokes
of memory. The farmhouse
seethes with lies and money,
the hushed greed for land
rising like the smell of something
dead. It is in the tinny
water. It is in the tasteless
food. And the old man's

dying is like icy breath
across the floor the others
wade through. Outside
all the tools are scattered
and the barn unfinished—
one wall like the pattern
of a jigsaw, shiplap ends
abstractly, chewed by air,
rafters already blue and veined,
gray stacks of two-by-fours
sinking in weeds.
The old house goes cold
then lumbers slowly
to another farm
leaving only echoes
and the scar
of its single footprint.
There is no end to this
seething. Back and forth,
climbing ladders of dust,
dreaming down cold valleys,
harvesting crops of ice.
I hear the music from Finn Hall:
The sound of feet and the secret
pint smuggled in the dark,
every fight a legend.

Farther west my father
packs potatoes—all those
lidless eyes in the huge
cellar—his shoulder rubbed
raw by the kitchen bulb,
the wound a gift brought back
from his vast travels
on wings of burlap
for fifty cents a day.
Later, bears move
in the summer trees. I feel
their huge poise, leafshade
their matted fur, tub
hearts thumping patience.
No corner can be turned.
Red eyes follow every
move. At night they
amble in, dark flanks
crowd the windows black,
rank breath snorts ashes
up the flue. Helpless,
I pray for winter—
for sleep, for the snows of sleep.
We move there now,
settling, tasting familiar dust,
travellers without tickets
thrown off the train,
hobos sapped crazy
by railroad bulls.

Moving West

The attempt to move west
Ends on the dry page
Meeting these words
And whatever loose map
The syntax scrawls
The journey is perpetual
Without punctuation
Only the place where lines
Stop
        or the mind
Pauses at crossroads
Stunned feeble
By choice
Every road becomes
The one not taken
(We back and fill
With allusion)
And of course
There should be passion
That show of feeling
When feeling snaps
Across the page
With asterisks
But the words refuse
Feeling is there with you

Inject some and make
The poem move west
With its own cutthroat
Manifest destiny
You can fill in the dead
You can supply the sweat
And even color in
The crazed eyes of the farm wife
With only one word
She never stops speaking
Alone Alone Alone Alone
Go on saying it
Until the whole wilderness
Of language falls around you
And then we will be together
There moving west
To clear our heads of words
In the ice of the Pacific

Lonely Roads
for Joan

What roads we followed, what interstates
of discontent, needle paths, pavements
pounded to flour to reach this room!
We trace them back tonight,
the surgical scar of that railroad,
a blue line of gravel through the hills.
We follow them all finding some tangled
as string in old drawers, unravelling
with ancient scarves, spread out
in our wrinkled palms, that relief
map of our lives. What dreams
brought us here? What fissures
have they crawled, what visions
of black light in the deepest fathoms
of our sleep? We trace them tonight,
each following a different route.
You go where you must—
the lonely Greyhound, five days
of cheese sandwiches, the half a house
where your childhood lives.
I move along the Columbia,
split off toward Ontario, Weiser, climbing
away from flat heat, dinosaur hills.
And as always New Meadows sleeps
except for the single light at the depot
left on for the bugs. Climbing
I uncover old anticipations like road signs,
catch that old taste of air, thin and clear,
the old house taking shape room by room,
the town rising around me
as I climb the stairs to you
flagging down your lonely Greyhound.

Carnegie-Mellon Poetry

1975
The Living and the Dead, Ann Hayes
In the Face of Descent, T. Alan Broughton

1976
The Week the Dirigible Came, Jay Meek
Full of Lust and Good Usage, Stephen Dunn

1977
*How I Escaped from the Labyrinth and
    Other Poems*, Philip Dacey
The Lady from the Dark Green Hills, Jim Hall
For Luck: Poems 1962-1977, H.L. Van Brunt
By the Wreckmaster's Cottage, Paula Rankin

1978
New & Selected Poems, James Bertolino
The Sun Fetcher, Michael Dennis Browne
A Circus of Needs, Stephen Dunn
The Crowd Inside, Elizabeth Libbey

1979
Paying Back the Sea, Philip Dow
Swimmer in the Rain, Robert Wallace
Far From Home, T. Alan Broughton
The Room Where Summer Ends, Peter Cooley
No Ordinary World, Mekeel McBride

1980
*And the Man Who Was Traveling Never Got
    Home*, H.L. Van Brunt
Drawing on the Walls, Jay Meek
The Yellow House on the Corner, Rita Dove
The 8-Step Grapevine, Dara Wier
The Mating Reflex, Jim Hall

1981
A Little Faith, John Skoyles
Augers, Paula Rankin
Walking Home from the Icehouse, Vern Rutsala